# Elton John Quiz Book

## 101 Questions To Test Your Knowledge Of This Incredibly Successful Musician

Published by Glowworm Press
7 Nuffield Way
Abingdon OX14 1RL
By Colin Carter

## Elton John Quiz

This book contains one hundred and one informative and entertaining trivia questions with multiple choice answers. With 101 questions, some easy, some more demanding, this entertaining book will really test your knowledge of Elton John.

You will be quizzed on a wide range of topics associated with Elton for you to test yourself; with questions on his early days, his songs, his lyrics, his achievements, his awards, his charity work and much more, guaranteeing you a truly educational experience. The Elton John Quiz Book will provide entertainment for fans of all ages, and will certainly test your knowledge of this world famous musician. The book is packed with information and is a must-have for all true Elton John fans, wherever you live in the world.

# FOREWORD

When I was asked to write a foreword to this book I was incredibly flattered.

I have known Colin for a number of years and his knowledge of facts and figures is phenomenal.

His love for music and his talent for writing quiz books makes him the ideal man to pay homage to the genius that is Sir Elton John.

This book came about as a result of a challenge during a round of golf!

I do hope you enjoy the book.


Terry Douglas

1. What was Elton John born as?
    A. Elton Dwight
    B. Kenneth Dwight
    C. Reginald Dwight
    D. Yorke Dwight

2. When was Elton born?
    A. 1945
    B. 1946
    C. 1947
    D. 1948

3. Where was Elton born?
    A. Barnet
    B. Harrow
    C. Pinner
    D. Ruislip

4. What middle name did Elton give himself?
    A. Apollo
    B. Hercules
    C. Neptune
    D. Zeus

5. When was Elton knighted by HM Queen Elizabeth II?
    A. 1996
    B. 1997
    C. 1998
    D. 1999

6. Who is Elton's long-time collaborator?

A. Benny Taupin
B. Bernie Taupin
C. Bertie Taupin
D. Billy Taupin

7. What was the name of Elton's first band?
A. Bluesology
B. Musicology
C. Rockology
D. Vulcanology

8. What is Elton's official website address?
A. elton.com
B. eltonjohn.com
C. officialelton.com
D. sireltonjohn.com

9. What is Elton's official twitter account?
A. @elton
B. @eltonjohn
C. @eltonofficial
D. @officialelton

10. What did President Macron of France present to Elton in June 2019?
A. Cesar Award
B. Grand Prix du Disque
C. Legion of Honour
D. Moliere Award

OK, so here are the answers to the first ten questions. If you get seven or more right, you are doing very well so far, but the questions will get harder.

A1. Elton was born as Reginald Kenneth Dwight.

A2. Elton was born on 25th March 1947.

A3. Elton was born in Pinner in Middlesex, England.

A4. Born Reginald Kenneth Dwight, he legally changed his name to Elton Hercules John on 7th January 1972.

A5. Elton was knighted by HM Queen Elizabeth II for "services to music and charitable services" in 1998. He thus became Sir Elton John. On receiving his knighthood Elton said, "I've had a long career and worked hard but I think the turning point came in 1990 when I got sober and started to do some charity work, particularly for the AIDS problem. A knighthood is the icing on the cake."

A6. Elton has worked with lyricist Bernie Taupin since 1967. They have collaborated on more than 30 albums.

A7. In 1962, at the age of 15 Elton joined a band called Bluesology. Their first recording session was in the Spring of 1965 with Elton aged just 18. The first single the band released was called Come Back,

Baby which was written and sung by Elton. It is worth tracking it down on YouTube for a piece of nostalgia and to hear his voice at such a tender age. Also in 1965 the band supported The Move at The Marquee Club on Wardour Street in London's Soho.

A8. eltonjohn.com is the official website. It provides a wealth of information including all the latest news, historical material and a complete discography.

A9. @eltonofficial is the official twitter account. It was set up in August 2010 and it tweets daily about news, and has almost a million followers.

A10. Elton was presented with the Legion of Honour (in French *Légion d'honneur)* by President Macron for his lifetime contribution to the arts and the fight against HIV. It is the highest French order of merit for military and civil merits, established in 1802 by Napoléon Bonaparte.

OK, back to the questions.

11. In which publication did Elton reply to an advert in 1967?
    A. Kerrang
    B. Melody Maker
    C. New Musical Express
    D. Sounds

12. What was Elton's debut single?
    A. Come Back Baby
    B. I've Been Loving You
    C. Love Me Always
    D. Your Song

13. What was Elton's debut album?
    A. Elton John
    B. Empty Sky
    C. This is Elton
    D. Tumbleweed Connection

14. When did Elton write "Your Song"?
    A. 1968
    B. 1969
    C. 1970
    D. 1971

15. How many studio albums did Elton record throughout the 1970s?
    A. 9
    B. 10
    C. 11

D. 12

16. Where did Elton play his first US gig?
    A. Trocadero
    B. Tropicana
    C. Troubadour
    D. Troubleshooter

17. What was the best-selling single from the album Honky Chateau album released in 1972?
    A. Daniel
    B. Honky Cat
    C. Rocket Man
    D. Tiny Dancer

18. What album was released in October 1973?
    A. Don't Shoot Me I'm Only The Piano Player
    B. Caribou
    C. Goodbye Yellow Brick Road
    D. Madman Across The Water

19. What was the name of Elton's Christmas single released in November 1973?
    A. Blue Christmas
    B. Calling It Christmas
    C. Step into Christmas
    D. Who'd be a Turkey at Christmas

20. In 1976, who sung the duet with Elton on "Don't Go Breaking My Heart"?

A. Kiki Dee
B. Gladys Knight
C. Ru Paul
D. Tammy Wynette

Here are the answers to the last set of questions.

A11. In June 1967, an advertisement appeared in New Musical Express, a British pop weekly paper, requesting applications from "artistes/composers singer-musicians". Both Elton John and Bernie Taupin applied, and Ray Williams who read their applications noticed their complementary talents and by putting the two talented men together he launched one of the greatest song writing partnerships in history.

A12. "I've Been Loving You" was Elton's debut single in 1968. The song's lyrics were originally credited to Bernie Taupin, although Elton later admitted that he wrote the entire song by himself, giving Taupin credit as an effort to earn Taupin his first publishing royalties. "I've Been Loving You" was not originally included on any album and the single was withdrawn shortly after its release. It did not appear on any official album release until the 1992 "Rare Masters" box set (which featured previously unreleased stereo mixes).

A13. "Empty Sky" was Elton's debut album. Although it was released in 1969 in the UK, it wasn't officially released in the US until 1975 and then with different artwork than the original release.

A14. Elton wrote "Your Song" on 27th October 1969. It was released a year later, and it was his first hit single. It has been certified platinum in the US and has been streamed over 100 million time son Spotify.

A15. Elton recorded an incredible total of 12 studio albums in the 1970s. The first album of the decade was the album self-titled Elton John. It has since been inducted into the Grammy Hall of Fame.

A16. Elton played his first US gig on 25th August 1970 at the Troubadour on Santa Monica Boulevard in Hollywood. In the 300 or so crowd that night was Neil Diamond.

A17. Rocket Man, the debut single from Elton's fifth studio album Honky Chateau, was released in April 1972.

A18. Goodbye Yellow Brick Road was released on 5th October 1973. Within a month, it had reached number 1 on the Billboard Top 200. The album includes Saturday Night's Alright (For Fighting), Bennie And The Jets and Candle In The Wind.

A19. Step into Christmas was recorded and released as a stand-alone single in November 1973. It is successful in its own right, and it also appears on many Christmas compilation albums.

A20. "Don't Go Breaking My Heart" is a duet by Elton John and Kiki Dee that was released in June 1976. Incredibly, it was the first number 1 single in the UK for Elton.  The song won the 1976 Ivor

Novello Award for Best Song Musically and Lyrically.

Here is the next set of questions.

21. In 1975 Elton covered what song by The Beatles?
    A. Back in the USSR
    B. Eleanor Rigby
    C. Lucy in the Sky with Diamonds
    D. Twist and Shout

22. At the Live Aid concert in 1985, who introduced Elton to the stage?
    A. Billy Connolly
    B. Bob Geldof
    C. John Hurt
    D. Rod Stewart

23. At the Live Aid concert in 1985, what was the first song that Elton sang?
    A. Bennie and the Jets
    B. Don't Let the Sun Go Down on Me
    C. I'm Still Standing
    D. Rocket Man

24. On the famous 1986 Australian tour, Elton dressed as which composer?
    A. Beethoven
    B. Mendelssohn
    C. Mozart
    D. Vivaldi

25. What was Elton's first number one solo single in the UK?

A.  Are You Ready For Love
B.  Crocodile Rock
C.  Honky Cat
D.  Sacrifice

26. Who designed the cover artwork for 1992's album "The One"?
A.  Giorgio Armani
B.  John Galliano
C.  Jean Paul Gaultier
D.  Gianni Versace

27. When was Elton indicted into the Rock and Roll Hall of Fame?
A.  1984
B.  1994
C.  2004
D.  2014

28. What Disney movie did Elton and Tim Rice compose the soundtrack for?
A.  Frozen
B.  The Jungle Book
C.  The Lion King
D.  Winnie the Pooh

29. Which song did Elton win an Oscar for in 1995?
A.  Be Prepared
B.  Can You Feel The Love Tonight
C.  Circle of Life
D.  Hakuna Matata

30. What was Elton's tribute to Diana Princess of Wales called?
   A. Candle in the Wind 1997
   B. Delightful Diana
   C. Never Forgotten
   D. Princess of Hearts

Here are the answers to the last set of questions.

A21. In November 1974, Elton released a cover version of Lucy in the Sky with Diamonds. It featured backing vocals and guitar by John Lennon.

A22. Scottish comedian Billy Connolly introduced Elton to the stage before his magnificent performance at the incredible Live Aid concert at Wembley Stadium on 13th July 1985.

A23. At Live Aid, Elton entered the stage at 8:50pm. He started with "I'm Still Standing" and he also performed "Bennie and the Jets", "Rocket Man", "Don't Go Breaking My Heart" (with Kiki Dee), "Don't Let the Sun Go Down on Me" (with Wham!) and finished with "Can I Get a Witness."

A24. From 5th November to 14th December 1976, Elton toured Australia with his band which was augmented by the 88 piece Melbourne Symphony Orchestra. The concerts featured Elton dressed as Mozart, complete with wig. The final show, at the Sydney Entertainment Centre, resulted in the live album "Live in Australia."

A25. Incredibly, the first number one that Elton had as a solo artist in the UK wasn't until 1990. His first UK number one solo single was "Sacrifice". The song got to the top of the charts in June 1990 and was at number one for a total of 5 weeks.

A26. The cover artwork for "The One" was designed by Gianni Versace. The album featured a duet with Eric Clapton, and a guitar solo from David Gilmour. The album sold over 2 million copies in the US alone.

A27. Elton was indicted into the Rock and Roll Hall of Fame on 19th January 1994 by Axl Rose, who said, "For myself, as well as many others, no one has been more of an inspiration than Elton John."

A28. The soundtrack to the movie The Lion King was written in collaboration with Tim Rice. The movie was released in 1994 and has become one of Disney's most successful, and most loved, movies of all time. The soundtrack to the movie has since gone on to sell over 15 million copies worldwide.

A29. Elton won an Oscar for Best Original Song for "Can You Feel The Love Tonight?" at the 1995 Academy Awards.

A30. Candle in the Wind 1997 was Elton and Bernie's heartfelt tribute to the late Diana, Princess of Wales. It has sold over 33 million copies, and has raised many millions for the Diana, Princess of Wales Memorial Fund. It is the highest selling single since charts began.

Here is the next set of questions.

31. What was Elton's concert residency in Las
    Vegas from 2004 to 2009 called?
    A. The Blue Piano
    B. The Red Piano
    C. The White Piano
    D. The Yellow Piano

32. What is Elton's husband's name?
    A. David Burnish
    B. David Furnish
    C. David Garnish
    D. David Varnish

33. What nationality is Elton's husband?
    A. American
    B. Australian
    C. Canadian
    D. Scottish

34. What is the first name of Elton's first son?
    A. Zachary
    B. Zander
    C. Zane
    D. Zavier

35. What was the name of the play that Elton
    provided music for in 2005?
    A. Billy Elliott
    B. Chicago
    C. Mamma Mia

D. Sunset Boulevard

36. Where was Elton's 60th birthday concert held?
    A. Hollywood Bowl, Los Angeles
    B. Madison Square Garden, New York City
    C. Red Rocks Amphitheatre, Colorado
    D. Stubbs, Austin

37. Which English football club is Elton associated with?
    A. Watford
    B. West Bromwich Albion
    C. West Ham United
    D. Wigan Athletic

38. Elton is famous for his world class collection of what?
    A. Antiques
    B. Photographs
    C. Stamps
    D. Watches

39. What is the song on Captain Fantastic and the Brown Dirt Cowboy album that has Biblical significance?
    A. The Dead Sea
    B. The Garden of Eden
    C. The Tower of Babel
    D. The Walls of Jericho

40. How many concerts has Elton performed in
    his career?
    A. Over 1,000
    B. Over 2,000
    C. Over 3,000
    D. Over 4,000

Here are the answers to the last block of questions.

A31. Conceived by Elton John and David LaChapelle, The Red Piano concert residency at The Colosseum at Caesars Palace in Las Vegas was originally planned as 75 shows over three years. When the curtains closed on the final show in March 2009, there had been 248 shows in total, grossing $169 million.

A32. Elton's husband is David Furnish. John proposed to Furnish in May 2005 and they entered into a civil partnership on 21st December 2005, the first day that civil partnerships could be performed in England. After same-sex marriage became legal in England in March 2014, John and Furnish retroactively converted their civil partnership into a marriage and marked the occasion with a ceremony in Windsor on 21st December 2014, the ninth anniversary of their civil partnership.

A33. David Furnish was born in Toronto in Canada in October 1962.

A34. Elton's first child, son Zachary Jackson Levon Furnish-John, was born in December 2010 in California via surrogacy. In January 2013, his second son, Elijah Joseph Daniel Furnish-John, was born through the same surrogate.

A35. Billy Elliot the Musical premiered at the Victoria Palace Theatre in London's West End on 11th May 2005. It closed on 9th April 2016, when the theatre closed for refurbishment, after 4,600 performances. The musical is based on the 2000 film and features music by Elton, with Lee Hall (who wrote the film's screenplay) providing the lyrics. The musical was performed in over twenty five countries, and it won 5 Laurence Olivier awards and 10 Tony awards.

A36. On 25th March 2007, Elton played a record breaking concert at Madison Square Garden in New York City to celebrate his 60th birthday. During the concert, he was joined on stage by Whoopi Goldberg and Robin Williams.

A37. Lifelong Watford supporter Elton became club chairman in 1976, at the age of 29. His tenure as chairman is remembered fondly by Watford supporters and he is now the Honorary Life President of the club. He has also used the club's ground as a venue for concerts. He first played at the stadium in 1974 and returned in 2005 and 2010 to stage fundraising concerts for the club.

A38. Over the past 25 years, Elton has put together one of the largest private collections of photography. In November 2016, over 150 pieces from his modernist collection, from more than 60 photographers including seminal figures such as Man Ray, Berenice Abbot, Alexandr Rodchenko and Edward Steichen, went on display at The Tate Modern in London.

A39. The Tower of Babel is a song from the 1975 album Captain Fantastic and the Brown Dirt Cowboy. The song contains these lines "It's party time for the guys in the Tower of Babel, Sodom meet Gomorrah, Cain meet Abel, Have a ball y'all".

A40. Since launching his first tour in 1970, Elton has made over 4,000 performances in more than 80 countries.

I hope you're having fun, and getting most of the answers right.

41. What is the name of the sports marketing business Elton founded in 2012?
    A. Rocket Enterprises
    B. Rocket Science Marketing
    C. Rocket Sports Management
    D. Rocket and Sprockett

42. When was the Elton John AIDS Foundation established?
    A. 1990
    B. 1992
    C. 1994
    D. 1996

43. Who is the drummer in Elton's band?
    A. Ray Cooper
    B. Davey Johnstone
    C. John Mahon
    D. Nigel Olsson

44. What was the name of the song Elton wrote for John Lennon?
    A. Cry to Heaven
    B. Empty Garden
    C. Funeral for a Friend
    D. Sacrifice

45. Where was Elton's ex-wife Renate Blauel born?

A. Austria
B. Germany
C. Hungary
D. Switzerland

46. When did Elton first perform in the USSR?
    A. 1973
    B. 1975
    C. 1977
    D. 1979

47. Philadelphia Freedom was written as a tribute to which tennis player?
    A. Chris Evert
    B. Julie Heldman
    C. Billie Jean King
    D. Martina Navratilova

48. Elton's version of Pinball Wizard featured in which film?
    A. Lifehouse
    B. Quadrophenia
    C. The Boy Who Heard Music
    D. Tommy

49. How many godchildren does Elton have?
    A. 6
    B. 8
    C. 10
    D. 12

50. Which song features a female Eastern European soldier in its promotional video?
    A. Healing Hands
    B. Nikita
    C. Sad Songs
    D. Wrap Her Up

Here are the answers to the last set of questions.

A41. In 2012, Elton founded Rocket Sports Management. It focuses on athlete management, brand sponsorships and consultancy. Amongst its many clients are Tour De France winner Geraint Thomas and multiple Olympic gold medal winning cyclist Laura Kenny.

A42. The Elton John AIDS Foundation was established by Elton in 1992 to support innovative HIV prevention, education programs, direct care and support services to people living with HIV. Elton was inspired to start the organization after losing two friends to AIDS in the span of a year. To date, it has raised over $400 million to support HIV related programs in fifty-five countries.

A43. There have been many band members over the years, but Nigel Olsson has played more than anyone else, having played more than 2,500 times with Elton. His first show was in April 1970, and he helped define the Elton John Band sound that took the singer's career to new heights in the 1970s and he has been an integral and much-loved part of the band for decades.

A44. Empty Garden (Hey Hey Johnny) is a song composed and performed by Elton, with lyrics by Bernie Taupin, which was written as a tribute to John Lennon, who had been assassinated 18 months earlier. It originally appeared on Elton's 1982 album Jump Up!

A45. Renate Blauel was born in Munich, Germany. She was a sound engineer, and the pair met in 1983 while Elton was finishing his Too Low for Zero album. The couple wed on Valentine's Day 1984 in Sydney, Australia and were married for four years.

A46. Elton played eight concerts in the Soviet Union (USSR)between 21st and 28th May 1979.  It was a significant event amid Cold War tensions between the USSR and the West at the time with the shows being among the first performed in the USSR by a Western pop star. In the 1970s, as with other Western artists, Elton's music was only available in the USSR via illegal import. Demand for the eight concerts was high, with ticket prices set at 8 roubles, which was about the average daily wage in the Soviet Union. Over 90 per cent of the tickets were taken by senior Communist Party members and military officers and the remainder were changing hands on the black market for up to 25 times the official price. It is worth tracking down a documentary entitled 'To Russia with Elton' on YouTube which is a fascinating insight into the period.

A47. Philadelphia Freedom was written in 1974 as a tribute to Billie Jean King who was part of the Philadelphia Freedoms professional tennis team at the time. The label on the vinyl for this record reads

"with Love to B.J.K. and the sound of Philadelphia."
At the time, King was ranked as the world's number
one women's tennis player. Elton and Billie-Jean
have since become good friends.

A48. Pinball Wizard was performed by Elton in the
1975 film adaptation of The Who's rock opera
Tommy. Elton's version in the film uses a piano as
the song's centerpiece in place of the acoustic guitar
in the original and features additional lyrics
specially written by Pete Townshend for the movie
version.

A49. Elton has ten godchildren, including John
Lennon's son Sean Lennon, model/actress Elizabeth
Hurley's son Damian Hurley and ex-footballer David
Beckham's sons Brooklyn and Romeo.

A50. Nikita is a successful love song which was
released in 1985.  The video for the song, directed
by Ken Russell, depicts Elton romancing a blonde
female East German border guard.

I hope you're learning some new facts about Elton, and here is the next set of questions.

51. What is the name of the 2019 movie biopic of Elton's life?
    A. The Bitch is Back
    B. Captain Fantastic
    C. Honky Cat
    D. Rocketman

52. Which actor played the part of Elton in the movie biopic?
    A. Jamie Bell
    B. Taron Egerton
    C. Tom Hardy
    D. Richard Madden

53. Which iconic woman was the subject of the original "Candle in the Wind"?
    A. Grace Kelly
    B. Jackie Kennedy
    C. Marilyn Monroe
    D. Natalie Wood

54. How many Grammy awards has Elton won?
    A. 2
    B. 3
    C. 4
    D. 5

55. Which song did George Michael duet with Elton?

A. Don't Let The Sun Go Down On Me
B. Goodbye Yellow Brick Road
C. Part Time Love
D. That's What Friends Are For

56. Which of these is a popular Elton John tribute act?
    A. Always Elton
    B. Endless Elton
    C. Forever Elton
    D. Ultimate Elton

57. Which of these 1960s classic did Elton play piano on?
    A. Friday On My Mind
    B. He Ain't Heavy He's My Brother
    C. Leaving On A Jet Plane
    D. Nights In White Satin

58. Which rapper did Elton score a number one single with in 2005?
    A. 2Pac
    B. Dr Dre
    C. Eminem
    D. Snoop Dogg

59. Which Strictly Come Dancing judge appeared on the music video for I'm Still Standing?
    A. Darcey Bussell
    B. Len Goodman
    C. Craig Revel Horwood
    D. Bruno Tonioli

60. Which song starts with the line 'Catch a star, if you can, wish for something special'?
    A. Are You Ready For Love
    B. Sorry Seems To Be The Hardest Word
    C. Tiny Dancer
    D. Your Song

Here are the answers to the last set of questions.

A51. Rocketman is a biographical musical film based on the life of Elton. The film was released in 2019 and received critical acclaim, with the story, the acting, the costume design and musical numbers receiving general praise.

A52. Taron Egerton played Elton John in the Rocketman movie. Additionally, Kit Connor and Matthew Illesley played Elton when he was a lot younger.

A53. Candle in the Wind was originally written in 1973, as a tribute to Marilyn Monroe, who had died 11 years earlier. The lyrics of the song are a sympathetic portrayal of her life and the song's opening line "Goodbye, Norma Jean" refers to Monroe's real name. In 1997, Elton performed a rewritten version of the song as a tribute to Diana, Princess of Wales.

A54. Elton has won five Grammy awards.

A55. In 1991, "Don't Let the Sun Go Down on Me" was covered in a live version as a duet by George Michael and Elton John. This version of the song had its greatest success. George Michael's Cover to Cover tour regularly included the song, and for the final show at Wembley Arena, London on 23rd March 1991, Michael brought out Elton as a surprise guest to sing it with him, and the live recording of this song, released as a single later that year, became a massive hit. The footage used for the single's music video was taken from a concert in Chicago and when Elton came out from the wings, the venue went crazy.

A56. There are a number of Elton tribute acts, but perhaps the best known is Ultimate Elton. While there can only be one Elton of course, Paul Bacon who brands himself as Ultimate Elton does a convincing job of looking and sounding like Elton. His Ultimate Elton tribute act is so popular, he typically plays over 100 gigs a year.

A57. Elton played piano on the recording of The Hollies 1969 hit He Ain't Heavy He's My Brother.

A58. Ghetto Gospel is a song by rapper 2Pac, also known as Tupac Shakur, which samples Elton's 1971 track, "Indian Sunset". The single topped the charts in Australia, Czech Republic, the Republic of Ireland and the United Kingdom The song was written by Tupac Shakur and was produced by Eminem.

A59. Bruno Tonioli, later a judge on the BBC's hit show Strictly Come Dancing and its American adaptation, Dancing with the Stars, appears as the leading male dancer in the video. To say he looks camp in the video would be an understatement.

A60. The opening lyrics 'Catch a star, if you can, wish for something special' are to "Are You Ready For Love?" which was originally recorded by Eton in 1977 and was originally produced in Philadelphia, and it was first released in the UK in 1979. In 2003, it was remixed and reached number 1 in the UK following his performing the song in a TV advert promoting the 2003–2004 football season for Sky Sports.

Let's give you some easier questions.

61. Which song starts with the line 'It's a little bit funny, this feeling inside'?
    A. Crocodile Rock
    B. Daniel
    C. Sorry Seems To Be The Hardest Word
    D. Your Song

62. Which song did the Beastie Boys cover in 1999?
    A. Bennie and the Jets
    B. Border Song
    C. Crocodile Rock
    D. Daniel

63. Which song literally translates as "No Worries"?
    A. Hakuna Matata
    B. Jambo Bwana
    C. Pumbaa Timon
    D. Wimoweh

64. What was the make of car mentioned in "Crocodile Rock"?
    A. Cadillac
    B. Chevrolet
    C. Chrysler
    D. Corvette

65. What Elton song describes the feelings of a Mars-bound astronaut?

A. Life on Mars
B. Rocket Man
C. Space Oddity
D. Starman

66. Where is Elton's primary residence when he is the UK?
   A. Old Cleeve
   B. Old Marston
   C. Old Windsor
   D. Old Woking

67. Where is Elton's primary residence when he is the USA?
   A. Atlanta
   B. Dallas
   C. New York City
   D. Phoenix

68. Which Queens of the Stone Age album does Elton feature on?
   A. ...Like Clockwork
   B. Era Vulgaris
   C. Lullabies to Paralyze
   D. Songs for the Deaf

69. Which song starts with the line 'You could never know what it's like'?
   A. I Guess That's Why They Call it the Blues
   B. I'm Still Standing
   C. Sorry Seems To Be The Hardest Word

D. Your Song

70. Which album did Saturday Night's Alright for Fighting first appear on?
   A. Captain Fantastic and the Brown Dirt Cowboy
   B. Don't Shoot Me I'm Only The Piano Player
   C. Goodbye Yellow Brick Road
   D. Honky Chateau

Here are the answers to the last ten questions.

A61. The opening lines 'It's a little bit funny this feeling inside; I'm not one of those who can easily hide. I don't have much money but boy if I did, I'd buy a big house where we both could live.' are to "Are You Ready For Love?" which was originally recorded by Eton in 1970.

A62. The Beastie Boys released a cover of Bennie and the Jets on their The Sounds of Science album in 1999. The song was sung by frequent Beastie Boys collaborator Biz Markie.

A63. Hakuna Matata is a song from The Lion King movie. The song is based on Timon the meerkat's catchphrase in the movie, Hakuna Matata, which is a Swahili phrase that means 'no worries'. If you ever travel in Kenya and Tanzania, you will hear the phrase a lot.

A64. It was a Chevrolet – and the slang version of it - Chevy. The song's opening verse is 'I remember when rock was young, Me and Suzie had so much fun, Holding hands and skimming stones, Had an old gold Chevy and a place of my own, But the biggest kick I ever got, Was doing a thing called the Crocodile Rock.'

A65. Rocket Man was recorded in 1972, and has become one of Elton's most loved singles. The song describes a Mars-bound astronaut's mixed feelings at leaving his family in order to do his job.

A66. Since 1975, the principal residence of Elton is a large detached house with 37 acres of gardens in Old Windsor, Berkshire, on the edge of Windsor Great Park. The house is called Woodside, and was originally built in the 18th century.

A67. Elton has a 6,000 square foot duplex apartment in Atlanta, Georgia. Rejecting Los Angeles as too overwhelming and New York as unsafe, he settled on a high-rise condominium in Atlanta, 36 floors above the madding crowd, explaining, "I like that Southern hospitality. Everyone is incredibly courteous and friendly."

A68. Elton appeared on the ...Like Clockwork album, which was released in 2013 by American rock band Queens of the Stone Age. Elton ended up on the album after surprising QOTSA lead singer Josh Homme with a phone call, telling him he needed an "actual queen" on the record. The album received critical acclaim and commercial success upon its release, reaching number two on the UK Albums Chart and number one on the Billboard 200 Chart in the United States.

A69. The opening lyrics 'You could never know what it's like, your blood like winter freezes just like ice' are to "I'm Still Standing" which was originally recorded by Elton in 1982 and released as a single in 1983. Elton said this song was "my reaction to still being relevant and successful in the early 1980s, post-punk and with the New-Romantics creeping in."

A70. Saturday Night's Alright For Fighting was originally released on the 1973 studio album Goodbye Yellow Brick Road and as the first single from the album. The song is one of Elton's most critically and commercially successful singles. Saturday Night's Alright for Fighting is a lively throwback to early rock and roll with a glam edge. The lyrics discuss a night out in town in which the narrator plans to "get about as oiled as a diesel train."

Here is the next set of questions.

71. Where did Elton study when he was young?
    A. The Royal Academy of Music
    B. The Royal College of Music
    C. The Royal Institute of Music
    D. The Royal School of Music

72. Who makes the pianos that Elton uses?
    A. Bechstein
    B. Moore and Moore
    C. Steinway
    D. Yamaha

73. Who did Elton duet with at the 2010 Grammy awards?
    A. Beyoncé
    B. Lady Gaga
    C. Madonna
    D. Mariah Carey

74. Where does Elton rank in the history of American charts in terms of most successful artists?
    A. 1st
    B. 3rd
    C. 6th
    D. 10th

75. 'Your Song' was featured in which film?
    A. Happy Feet
    B. Moulin Rouge!

C. Strictly Ballroom
D. Toy Story

76. Who inspired the album title 'Don't Shoot Me I'm Only The Piano Player'?
    A. Billy Joel
    B. Liberace
    C. Groucho Marx
    D. Freddie Mercury

77. Which live version of a Beatles song was recorded by Elton John and John Lennon in 1974?
    A. All You Need Is Love
    B. Come Together
    C. I Saw Her Standing There
    D. Twist And Shout

78. In the song Daniel, where are the red tail lights heading for?
    A. England
    B. France
    C. Germany
    D. Spain

79. Which album, released in 1971, included the songs Levon and Tiny Dancer?
    A. Elton John
    B. Honky Chateau
    C. Madman Across The Water
    D. Tumbleweed Connection

80. Who is the record producer most associated
with Elton John?
   A. Gus Dudgeon
   B. Stuart Epps
   C. Kevin McCollum
   D. Ray Williams

Here are the answers to the last set of questions.

A71. At the age of 11 Elton won a junior scholarship to the Royal Academy of Music in central London where he attended Saturday classes for five years. Several instructors have attested that he was a model student.

A72. Elton has used Yamaha Disklavier grand pianos exclusively since he first played one many years ago. "When it comes to my piano," he says, "Yamaha shares my philosophy that anything short of perfect simply isn't good enough."

A73. Lady Gaga and Sir Elton John provided the highlight of the 2010 Grammy Awards with a piano duet as they traded verses on Speechless and Your Song. Elton had previously performed a Grammy duet in 2001, when he sang with Eminem.

A74. Elton is the third most successful artist in the history of American charts – behind only Elvis Presley and The Beatles.

A75. Your Song was featured in the film Moulin Rouge! Ewan McGregor sang it as he was wooing Nicole Kidman.

A76. The title of 'Don't Shoot Me I'm Only The Piano Player' came from a meeting with Groucho Marx. He befriended Elton when the singer was staying in California in 1972, with Groucho insisting on calling him "John Elton." When Groucho jokingly pointed his index fingers as if holding a pair of six-shooters, Elton put up his hands and said, "Don't shoot me, I'm only the piano player," thereby naming the album he had just completed. A film poster for the Marx Bros. movie Go West is on the album cover in homage to Groucho. The album was a huge hit on both sides of the Atlantic, topping the UK and US album charts.

A77. The live recording of I Saw Her Standing There was issued in February 1975 as the B-side to Elton's single Philadelphia Freedom. The recording came from a memorable concert at Madison Square Garden on 28th November 1974. Lennon's onstage appearance was unannounced prior to the event, and the crowd reaction was ecstatic. Lennon wore a black suit, and performed three songs with Elton, opening with Whatever Gets You Thru The Night and following with versions of Lucy In The Sky With Diamonds and I Saw Her Standing There. Sadly, the show was Lennon's last appearance before a paying audience.

A78. The opening lyrics to Daniel are 'Daniel is travelling tonight on a plane; I can see the red tail lights heading for Spain.' The song was recorded in 1972 and released as a single in 1973.

A79. Levon and Tiny Dancer appear on Madman Across the Water which was the fourth studio album released by Elton.

A80. Gus Dudgeon was the producer most closely associated with the production of many of Elton's most acclaimed recordings. Elton later proclaimed him the greatest producer of his generation and credited him with spurring on his career.

Here are the next set of questions, let's hope you get most of them right.

81. Where is the 'blue jean baby' on Tiny Dancer from?
    A. La Jolla
    B. Las Vegas
    C. Los Angeles
    D. Los Gatos

82. Which female singer recorded a cover version of The Bitch is Back?
    A. Britney Spears
    B. Cher
    C. Mariah Carey
    D. Tina Turner

83. What was the name of the documentary film made about Elton by David Furnish in 1997?
    A. Clowns & Crowns
    B. Hair & Headdresses
    C. Moods & Music
    D. Tantrums & Tiaras

84. Who is the percussionist in Elton's band?
    A. Billy Cooper
    B. Ray Cooper
    C. Simon Cooper
    D. Tommy Cooper

85. What is the name of the function that Elton has run for over twenty years to support his AIDS foundation?
    A. Mid Summer's Night Party
    B. Moonlight Madness
    C. Opal Fashion Show
    D. White Tie and Tiara Ball

86. Which war is the song Daniel about?
    A. Crimean War
    B. Korean War
    C. Second World War
    D. Vietnam War

87. Which song contains the line 'I never knew me a better time, and I guess I never will.'?
    A. Crocodile Rock
    B. Daniel
    C. I Guess That's Why They Call it the Blues
    D. Saturday Night's Alright For Fighting

88. Which of these is not an Elton John album?
    A. Ballad of a Well Known Gun
    B. Caribou
    C. Made in England
    D. Too Low For Zero

89. Which of these songs is a tribute to John Lennon?
    A. Ballad of a Well Known Gun
    B. Empty Garden

C. Made in England
D. Too Low For Zero

90. Who wrote the lyrics to 'Blue Eyes'?
   A. Barry Osborne
   B. Gary Osborne
   C. Harry Osborne
   D. Larry Osborne

Here are the answers to the last set of questions.

A81.The opening lyrics to Tiny Dancer are 'Blue jean baby, L.A. lady, seamstress for the band, Pretty eyed, pirate smile, you'll marry a music man.' The L.A. lady is thus from Los Angeles. The lyrics are by Elton's song writing partner, Bernie Taupin. He actually married the band's seamstress, named Maxine in 1971, with Elton serving as his best man. Maxine went on to design a number of the flamboyant stage costumes that Elton wore at the time.

A82. Tina Turner recorded The Bitch is Back twice – once for her Rough album in 1978, and again for the tribute album Two Rooms in 1991. Turner also often performed the song in her live show. The idea for the song was inspired by Bernie Taupin's wife at the time, Maxine Feibelman, who would say, "The bitch is back," when John was in a bad mood. Elton later commented, "It is kind of my theme song."

A83. Tantrums & Tiaras is the name of the 1997 documentary film about Elton, directed by David Furnish. It features unprecedented access into one of the world's greatest musical talents and his larger than life lifestyle. It is a fascinating and honest look at Elton the man rather than Elton the musician. A DVD from 2008 with commentary from Elton is available on Amazon.

A84. Percussionist Ray Cooper has been a full- and part-time member of the Elton John Band since 1971. Ray studied classical piano as a youth, then strings and woodwinds, and later, percussion. He has played on hits by America (A Horse With No Name), Carly Simon (You're So Vain) and David Essex (Rock On), as well as on many other projects. Cooper makes a lasting impression on fans every time he picks up an instrument on stage with his rambunctious stage persona.

A85. For over twenty years, Elton has opened the doors to his Old Windsor home for an Annual White Tie and Tiara Ball to raise funds for the Elton John AIDS Foundation. Over the years over £50 million has been raised at the balls.

A86. Daniel is one of Elton's most misunderstood songs. Bernie Taupin wrote the lyrics to Daniel in 1973 after reading an article about a Vietnam War veteran who had been wounded, and wanted to get away from the attention he was receiving when he went back home. He explained, "The story was about a guy that went back to a small town in Texas, returning from the Vietnam War. They'd lauded him when he came home and treated him like a hero. But, he just wanted to go home, go back to the farm, and try to get back to the life that he'd led before. I wanted to write something that was sympathetic to the people that came home."

A87. The line 'I never knew me a better time, and I guess I never will' is from Crocodile Rock, written and recorded in 1972.

A88. The odd one out is Ballad of a Well Known Gun. This is the opening track from the Tumbleweed Connection album.

A89. Empty Garden (Hey Hey Johnny) is a song written as a tribute to John Lennon, who had been assassinated 18 months earlier. It originally appeared on Elton's 1982 album Jump Up!. The song title "Empty Garden" refers to the huge pile of flowers left behind by mourners outside The Dakota, Lennon's home in New York City, near the site where he was assassinated.

A90. Gary Osborne wrote the lyrics to Blue Eyes, a huge hit in 1982 for Elton. He also co-wrote Part Time Love and Little Jeannie. Osborne is a very talented guy and he was the principal lyricist on Jeff Wayne's Musical Version of The War of the Worlds album which has sold in excess of 15 million albums.

Here is the final set of questions. Enjoy!

91. Where did the album Caribou get its name from?
    A. An inuit group in Canada
    B. A ranch in Colorado
    C. A rum based drink
    D. A type of coffee

92. Which song on the Goodbye Yellow Brick Road album is entirely instrumental?
    A. Funeral for a Friend
    B. Roy Rogers
    C. Social Disease
    D. Sweet Painted Lady

93. Which song was a tribute to a messenger who was killed in a motorcycle accident?
    A. Big Dipper
    B. Georgia
    C. Return to Paradise
    D. Song For Guy

94. Elton's song Amoreena accompanied the credits to which film?
    A. Bobby Deerfield
    B. Carlito's Way
    C. Dog Day Afternoon
    D. Scarface

95. Which song contains the lines 'I'm better than you. It's the way that I move. The things that I do'?
    A. Healing Hands
    B. Kiss The Bride
    C. Little Jeanie
    D. The Bitch Is Back

96. What is the name of the song on the album "Jump Up" that is also a famous war novel?
    A. All Quiet On The Western Front
    B. For Whom The Bell Tolls
    C. The Quiet American
    D. War and Peace

97. What album featured the single Island Girl?
    A. A Single Man
    B. Blue Moves
    C. Rock of the Westies
    D. Victim of Love

98. What is Elton's most successful album of all time?
    A. Elton John
    B. Elton John's Greatest Hits
    C. Goodbye Yellow Brick Road
    D. The One

99. Which song contains the lines 'You called out to our country, and you whispered to those in pain'?
    A. Candle in the Wind 1997

B. Healing Hands
C. Kiss The Bride
D. Little Jeanie

100.    What is the name of Elton's final ever tour?
    A. Farewell My Concubines
    B. Farewell To Arms
    C. Farewell To You All
    D. Farewell Yellow Brick Road

101.    Where will Elton play his last concert in 2020 on his Farewell Tour?
    A. London
    B. Paris
    C. New York
    D. Sydney

Here are the answers to the last set of questions.

A91. Caribou Ranch was a recording studio built in a converted barn on ranch property in the Rocky Mountains, on the road that leads to the ghost town of Caribou in Colorado. Elton's 1974 album Caribou was recorded at and named after the studio.

A92. Funeral for a Friend is the only track on Goodbye Yellow Brick Road that is entirely instrumental  It was created by Elton while he was thinking of what kind of music he would like at his own funeral. This song is frequently the opening number in Elton's concerts.

A93. "Song For Guy" from the 1978 album "A Single Man" was a tribute to the band's 17 year old messenger Guy Burchette who was killed in a motorcycle accident. It is manly instrumental but it has an emotional line at the end, which when heard is never forgotten – "Life isn't everything." It was a commercial success worldwide except for in the U.S., where instrumental hits are rare.

A94. Amoreena is a song from the 1970 album Tumbleweed Connection. The song accompanied the opening credits of the 1975 film Dog Day Afternoon which starred Al Pacino as an inexperienced criminal who leads a bank robbery in Brooklyn, with things quickly going wrong. Amoreena is also the name of John's god-daughter.

A95. The lyrics "I'm better than you. It's the way that I move. The things that I do" are from "The Bitch is Back". Its title was contentious when it was released in 1974 with several radio stations in the United States and elsewhere refusing to play the song because of the word "bitch". Elton responded to the controversy, quipping, "Some radio stations in America are more puritanical than others."

A96. All Quiet On The Western Front is the closing track of Elton's 1982 album Jump Up!. All Quiet On The Western Front is a classic war novel written in 1929 by Erich Maria Remarque and it describes a generation destroyed by war.

A97. Island Girl was the first single taken from the album Rock of the Westies. The lyrics to the song are about a prostitute in New York City and a man who wants to take her back to Jamaica.

A98. Elton has recorded 30 studio albums, 4 live albums, 7 soundtrack albums, 16 compilation albums, as well as 2 other albums, selling more than 200 million albums worldwide. His biggest selling studio album is Goodbye Yellow Brick Road, which has sold more than 31 million copies worldwide to date.

A99. The lyrics 'You called out to our country, and you whispered to those in pain, now you belong to heaven, and the stars spell out your name.' are to

Candle in the Wind 1997, Elton's heartfelt tribute to the late Diana, Princess of Wales.

A100. After more than half a century on the road and an unparalleled career that has redefined the cultural landscape and seen him claim his place as a true global icon, Elton is playing his final ever tour called 'Farewell Yellow Brick Road'. Running from September 2018, the Farewell Yellow Brick Road tour will consist of more than 300 shows across five continents, hitting North America, Europe and the Middle East, Asia, South America and Australasia.

A101. Elton's farewell tour finishes in December 2020, with his final concert being at the O2 in London. It is hard to believe that this will be Elton's last ever tour performance. I have tickets, and I know it's going to be a very emotional night.

That's it. I hope you enjoyed this book, and I hope you got most of the answers right. I also hope you learnt a few new things about Sir Elton.

If you saw anything wrong, or if you have any comments, please get in touch via the glowwormpress.com website.

Thanks for reading, and if you did enjoy the book, please leave a positive review on Amazon.

Made in the USA
Middletown, DE
28 December 2019